**DO NOT REMOVE
CARDS FROM POCKET**

5/85

Sports Stars

CARL LEWIS

The Second Jesse Owens

By Bert Rosenthal

CHILDRENS PRESS ™

CHICAGO

Cover photograph: Dan Honda
Inside photographs courtesy of the following:
Victor G. Sailer, pages 7, 9, 13, 17, 19, 21, 31, 33, 35, 37, 39, and 42
Greg Sailer, page 11
Pineda/Sailer, page 15
Chuck Muhlstock, page 25
Al Messerschmidt, page 28

Library of Congress Cataloging in Publication Data

Rosenthal, Bert.
  Carl Lewis: the second Jesse Owens.

  (Sport stars)
  Summary: A biography of the New Jersey son of track-
coach parents, holder of world records as a sprinter and long
jumper, who won the Jesse Owens Award in 1982 and three
medals in Helsinki in 1983.
  1. Lewis, Carl, 1961-   —Juvenile literature.
2. Track and field athletes—United States—Biography—
Juvenile literature. [1. Lewis, Carl, 1961-   . 2. Track and
field athletes. 3. Afro-Americans—Biography]
I. Title. II. Series.

GV697.L48R67 1984   796.4'2'0924 [B] [92] 83-23984
ISBN 0-516-04336-6

1 2 3 4 5 6 7 8 9 10 11 12 R 91 90 89 88 87 86 85 84

Sports Stars

CARL LEWIS

The Second Jesse Owens

Carl Lewis was born to be an athlete.

His father, Bill, was an athlete. When Bill was younger, he played football. He also competed in track and field. His best events were the sprint and the long jump.

Carl's mother, Evelyn, also was an athlete. She also competed in track and field. Her best event was the hurdles. In 1951, Evelyn was a member of a United States team. The team competed in the Pan American Games. Evelyn finished sixth in the 80-meter hurdles.

Carl's oldest brother, Mackie, also was an athlete. Mackie liked track and field, too. Like his father, his best events were the sprint and long jump.

Carl's second oldest brother is named Cleve. He also was an athlete. His favorite sport, however, was soccer. He was an All-America soccer player at Brandeis University. Later, he was drafted by a pro team. That team was the Cosmos. Cleve was the first American black player to be drafted by a pro soccer team.

Carl also has a younger sister, Carol. Like her brothers, she is an athlete. Her Number 1 sport is track and field. Her best events are the hurdles and the long jump.

But the best athlete in the family is Carl. He is a star in track and field. He is the world's best sprinter and long jumper.

Carl became interested in the sport when he was very young. The interest began because of his mother and father. They brought up their four children around the track. Bill and Evelyn started a track club. It was in Willingboro, New Jersey, where they lived. Bill and Evelyn coached the club team.

When Carl was seven years old, he began hanging around the club. So did Carol. She was only five then.

When Carl was 10, he competed in a Jesse Owens age-group meet. The meet was in Philadelphia. (Jesse Owens was one of the greatest track and field athletes in history. His best events were the sprint, the hurdles, and the long jump.)

Owens was Bill Lewis' hero. Jesse lived and worked in Chicago in the 1940s. At the time, Bill Lewis went to school there. He went to Dunbar Vocational School.

"Jesse was always my superhero," said Bill. "I never met a man I was so impressed with."

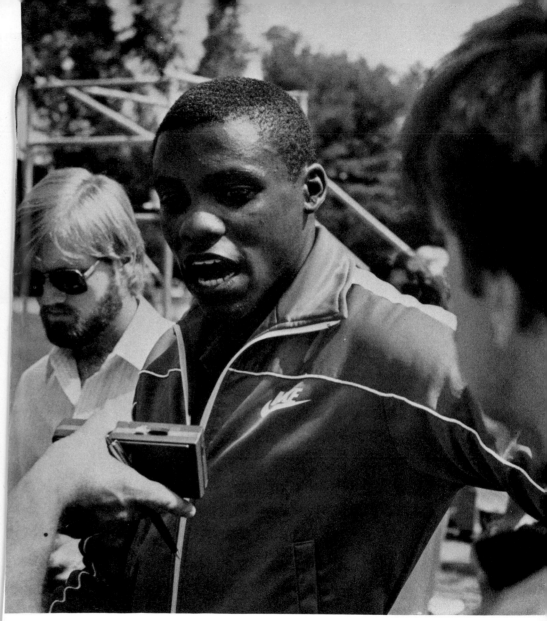

Carl is very much at ease when he is being interviewed.

"We just wanted to have fun while they were coaching," said Carl. "There was no pressure from our parents. We could have fun competing in any event we wanted. The long jump just grew on both of us."

When Carl was nine, he began competing. Carol started when she was seven.

"Carol and a friend won an age-group meet by themselves one time," Carl said. "I think Carol won five events."

Carol was younger than her brother. But she was the better athlete at the time.

"Everybody in my family showed potential but me," said Carl. "I was the ugly duckling. I felt left out. But I stuck with it."

Carl, his sister Carol, and Stephanie Hightower, one of Ameri high hurdlers, cheer on one of their teammates.

At the age-group meet, Bill took Carl to meet Jesse. They all talked for a short time. Bill thinks that meeting Jesse helped Carl become a good long jumper.

But Carl said, "Nobody was into the long jump. So I always had a lot of time to practice. I never had to wait my turn. I got to run and jump."

Carl ran and jumped because he liked doing those things. His parents did not make him do them.

"We just tried to let him grow up," said Carl's father. "We didn't shove track in his face. We didn't put pressure on him to be great."

Carl's coach Tom Tellez

But Carl's mother and father did help him. They coached him a lot.

"There's a very thin line when you're coaching your own kids," said Bill Lewis. "You can make or break them."

The Lewises made Carl. They did not break him. Some parents can break a child by pushing too hard. It happens a lot in Little League baseball.

"Most Little League parents aren't trained as coaches," said Bill Lewis. "We are. It helped."

Bill added, "We had a together kind of situation. We did everything as a family."

Carol also competes in the long jump.

Meanwhile, Carol was moving ahead faster than Carl. When Carl was in the ninth grade, he long jumped 19 feet, 11 inches. When Carol was in the ninth grade, she long jumped 20 feet, 5 inches.

Track and field was not Carol's only sport. She liked diving, gymnastics, and basketball.

Carol competed in those sports only for fun. It was something different to do. Best of all, she liked track and field. She liked it because Carl liked it. Carol was Carl's friend. They did a lot of things together.

His friends were her friends. She played their games. Carl and Carol were always together.

Carl's three events are the 100 meters, the 200 meters, and the long jump.

Carl took cello lessons. He also played in the school orchestra.

Carol took violin lessons. She also played in the school orchestra.

Carl wanted to be a long jumper. So did Carol.

When Carl was only seven years old, Bob Beamon set the world long jump record. His distance was 29 feet, 2½ inches. Bob's record jump came in the 1968 Olympic Games. His jump was nearly two feet longer than anyone ever had jumped.

It was a very long jump.

Carl was too young to really understand what Bob had done. But when Carl was 11, he read about Bob's great jump. He wondered just how far it was.

So Carl took a tape measure and measured the distance. He measured it in his front yard.

"My goodness," said Carl. "That's a long way."

It was such a long way that many people didn't think the record ever would be broken. It seemed so far out of reach. In one way, it was good for long jumping. In another way, it was bad.

It was good because it was such a great jump. It was bad because no one thought it could be broken. So many track athletes didn't want to long jump. They tried other events. So, the long jump became almost a forgotten event.

But Carl Lewis didn't forget it. He started chasing Bob's record.

At the age of 12, Carl long jumped 17 feet, 6 inches. A year later, he had reached 18 feet, 1 inch. When he was 14, his best was 19 feet, 11 inches. Carl was improving very fast.

The next year, Carl entered high school. The name of the school was Willingboro High School. His mother coached the girls' track team there.

Carl's father and mother are track coaches. His parents coached him when he was young. Now they cheer for him when he runs.

Carl's father also is a girls' track coach. He is the coach at Kennedy High School.

In high school, Carl was a long jumper and hurdler. In his first year, he long jumped 22 feet, 9 inches. That broke the school record.

After that, Carl set a goal. His goal was to jump 25 feet before he was out of high school. He even put the number 25 on his jacket. Some of the other students laughed at him. They didn't think he would be able to do it.

Carl didn't think it was funny. He was going to show them that it could be done.

In his second year, Carl also was on his school's hurdles relay team. A relay team usually is made up of four runners. It was one of the best teams in south Jersey. In the state meet, it was going for a title.

When Carl ran in the state relay race, he did poorly. He hit five of the 10 hurdles. He lost the race.

When he came off the track, a teammate told him: "You'll never be a good athlete. You're not running relays with us again."

Carl was sad. He was unhappy. But he didn't give up hurdling that year.

However, he did give it up in his third year in high school. That was the year he began sprinting. He began sprinting just to help his team get

some points in the state meet. By the end of the season, his time for the 100-yard dash was 9.8 seconds.

Carl found it easier to long jump and sprint than to long jump and hurdle. So he made a deal with his coach. They agreed that if Carl could run 9.5 seconds for the 100, he would not have to hurdle in his senior year. By the end of the summer in his junior year, he got his 100-yard time down to 9.3 seconds.

Carl also reached his other goal. He long jumped 25 feet, 9 inches.

Now, Carl was a long jumper and a sprinter instead of a long jumper and a hurdler.

Between his junior year and the time he entered the University of Houston, Carl got his long jump distance to 26 feet, 8 inches. He also made two United States teams. One was the 1979 Pan American team. It was the same team his mother had been on 28 years earlier.

The other team was one that competed in a big meet in Russia. In both meets Carl finished third in the long jump. For that, he got two bronze medals.

Then, it was time to go to Houston.

"When I started college, people said I couldn't long jump and run the 100, too," said Carl.

He told them: "I'm a long jumper and a sprinter both."

Carl proved he could do well in both events. He didn't do well only against other college athletes. He did well against the best athletes in the world.

During his freshman year at Houston, Carl won two national collegiate long jump titles. They were at the indoor and outdoor meets.

After his freshman year, Carl competed in the United States Olympic Trials. He was in two events. They were the long jump and the sprint. He made the team in two events. In the long jump, he finished second. In the 100-meter dash, he finished fourth. That earned him a place on the sprint-relay team.

Carl was not the only member of the Lewis family to make the team. His sister, Carol, also made it. She did it by finishing third in the women's long jump.

"When Carol made it, it was a bigger thrill than when I did," said Carl.

Carl was only 18 years old then. Carol was just 16.

However, Carl and Carol did not compete in the Olympics that year. They didn't compete because the United States didn't compete. That was on orders from President Carter. The Games that year were in Russia. Russia had invaded Afganistan. President Carter didn't like that. So he ordered the United States team to stay home.

Carl shakes hands with Ray Lumpp, a former basketball player who is head meet director of U.S. Olympic Invitational.

That didn't stop Carl from improving as a long jumper and a sprinter.

In his second—or sophmore—year in college, Carl was outstanding.

Indoors, he won the national collegiate long jump and sprint titles. No other athlete ever had won these events in the same year in the meet's history. He also got off the best long jump in indoor history. That was 27 feet, 10¼ inches.

Outdoors, Carl also won the national collegiate long jump and sprint titles. Only two others had done it before him in the meet's 60-year history. The last had been Jesse Owens in 1935 and 1936.

Carl sets the sea-level record for the long jump outdoors by jumping
28 feet, 9 inches.

Carl also won the national long jump and sprint titles. The last athlete to do it was Jesse Owens in 1936.

In addition, Carl ran the 100-meter dash in 10.0 seconds. That was the fastest time ever at sea level. The world record of 9.95 seconds was set at a higher altitude by Jim Hines of the United States. He did it at the 1968 Olympic Games in Mexico City.

Carl also long jumped 28 feet, 3½ inches. That was the best jump ever at sea level. Bob Beamon's record of 29 feet, 2½ inches also was set at a higher altitude in the Olympic Games in Mexico City.

Carl waits to be interviewed by Ralph Boston, a former world record holder in the long jump, and a newswoman from ESPN.

Carl also finished first that year in the long jump at the World Cup meet. That meet brought together the best track and field athletes in the world.

For doing all those things, Carl was named the outstanding amateur athlete in the United States in 1981. In honor of it, he received the Sullivan Award.

But Carl didn't stop there.

In his senior year, he broke his indoor long jump record. This time, he went 28 feet, 1 inch. He also won the national indoor long jump title. Outdoors, he won the national long jump and sprint titles for the second year in a row. The last man to do that was Malcolm Ford in 1884-85.

Carl also long jumped 28 feet, 9 inches. That broke the record for a jump at sea level. It also

was only 5½ inches short of Bob Beamon's world record.

Carl also tied his sea-level record for the 100-meter dash. For the second year in a row, he ran the distance in 10.0 seconds.

Also, for the second year in a row, he was ranked Number 1 in the world in the long jump and the sprint. Carl also was named winner of the Jesse Owens Award for 1982. That is given to the outstanding track and field performer of the year.

Carl continued to shine in 1983. Indoors, he ran the fastest-ever 60-yard dash. His time was 6.02 seconds. Outdoors, he ran the 100-meter dash in 9.96 seconds. It was the fastest ever at sea level. It was only one-hundredth of a second off Jim Hines' record.

In August of 1983 Carl competed in the world championships in Helsinki, Finland. He entered three events.

In the 100-meter race, Carl was first with a time of 10.07 seconds. In the long jump Carl won with a jump of 28 feet, ¾ inches.

Then Carl, Emmit King, Willie Gault, and Calvin Smith ran the 400-meter relay. Carl was the anchor (or last) man in the race. They won in 37.86 seconds. They set a world record.

Carl now had three more medals—all gold.

"I want to be the best of all time," said Carl. "The best sprinter. The best long jumper."

CHRONOLOGY

1961—Carl Lewis is born on July 1 in Birmingham, Alabama.

1963—Carl and the Lewis family move to Willingboro, New Jersey.

1970—At the age of 9, Carl begins his track and field career.

1971—Carl competes in his first Jesse Owens meet.

1976—Carl breaks his high school record in the long jump, leaping 22 feet, 9 inches.

1977—Carl breaks the record again, going 23 feet, 10 inches.

1978—For the third year in a row, Carl breaks the long jump record, going 25 feet, 9 inches. He also begins his sprinting career.

1979—This year, Carl long jumps 26 feet, 8 inches. He also wins two bronze medals in international meets. The bronze medals are for finishing third each time.

1979—Carl enters the University of Houston.

1980—Carl wins the national collegiate outdoor long jump title.

—Carl makes the United States Olympic team as a long jumper and a relay runner.

1981—Carl wins the national collegiate indoor long jump and sprint titles. He also wins the national collegiate outdoor long jump and sprint titles. He gets a third "double" this year by winning the national long jump and sprint outdoor titles.

—Carl records the best indoor long jump in history—27 feet, 10¼ inches. He records the best outdoor long jump at sea level—28 feet, 3½ inches. He runs the fastest-ever 100-meter dash at sea level—10.0 seconds.

—Carl wins the Sullivan Award as the nation's outstanding amateur athlete.

1982—Carl sets the indoor long jump record again, going 28 feet, 1 inch. He sets the sea-level record for the long jump outdoors, going 28 feet, 9 inches. He ties his sea-level record for the 100-meter dash, running 10.0 seconds.

—Carl wins the Jesse Owens Award as the outstanding track and field performer of the year.

1983—Carl breaks the indoor record for the 60-yard dash—6.02 seconds. He runs the fastest-ever 100-meter dash at sea level—9.96 seconds.

—In Helsinki Carl wins three gold medals. He wins the 100-meter race in 10.07 seconds and is first in the long jump with a jump of 28 feet, ¾ inches. He anchors the U.S. relay team and they win with a record-breaking time of 37.86 seconds.

ABOUT THE AUTHOR

Bert Rosenthal has worked for The Associated Press for more than 25 years. He has covered or written about virtually every sport. Mr. Rosenthal is the author of Sports Stars books on Larry Bird, Marques Johnson, Sugar Ray Leonard, Darryl Dawkins, Wayne Gretzky, and Isiah Thomas. He also is the author of New True Books on Soccer and Basketball.

He was AP's pro basketball editor from 1973 until 1976. From 1974 until 1980, he was the secretary-treasurer of the Professional Basketball Writers' Association of America. He has been a co-author on two books—*Pro Basketball Superstars of 1974* and *Pro Basketball Superstars of 1975*. For seven years Mr. Rosenthal was an editor of *HOOP Magazine*, an official publication of the National Basketball Association.

At present, he is the AP's track and field editor, and a frequent contributor to many basketball, football, and baseball magazines. He also has covered two Olympic Games—the 1976 Olympics at Montreal and the 1980 Games at Moscow.